YELLOW ARROW

Vol. IX, No. 1
Spring 2024
Elevate

Yellow Arrow Journal

Creative nonfiction, poetry, and cover art by writers and
artists identifying as women

Vol. IX, No. 1
Spring 2024
Elevate

Editor-in-Chief
Kapua Iao

Guest Editor
Jennifer N. Shannon

Editorial Associates and Readers
Sydney Alexander, Jill Earl, Angela Firman, Meg Gamble,
Amaya Lambert, Siobhan McKenna, Samantha Pomerantz,
Kait Quinn, Leticia Priebe Rocha, Nicky Ruddell,
Mel Silberger, and Beck Snyder

Contributors
brooklyn baggett, Ellen Blum Barish, Daisy Bassen,
Elliott batTzedek, Rachel R. Baum, Robin Dellabough,
Michele Evans, Jennifer Martinelli Eyre, Bridget Hayes,
Elizabeth Hill, Jean Janicke, Carter Lappin, Rebecca D. Martin,
Glenis Moore, Mary Moreno, Jordan Eve Morral, Sara Palmer,
Sarah Piper, Shieva Salehnia, Susan Shea, Morgan Sheehan,
Tramaine Suubi, Annabelle Taghinia, Bethany Tap,
Angelica Terso, Ann Weil, Melanie Weldon-Soiset,
Samantha Liana Williams, and Cathy Wittmeyer

Cover Art
Lizzie Brown

YELLOW ARROW

PUBLISHING

PO Box 65185, Baltimore, MD 21209
info@yellowarrowpublishing.com

Yellow Arrow Journal - Elevate
Copyright © 2024 by Yellow Arrow Publishing
All rights reserved.

ISBN (paperback): 979-8-9883176-2-3
ISSN (print): 2688-3015
ISSN (online): 2688-3023

Cover art by Lizzie Brown.
Cover and interior design by Yellow Arrow Publishing.
For more information, see yellowarrowpublishing.com.

Table of Contents

Cicada
Elliott batTzedek

Whatever cannot grow,
whatever restricts—
peel it off.

Even skin must split,
crack open, give way,
when you force
your way out. Even if it slices,
even if this leaves you raw
and wet
and strange.

Look back. How little it was,
your confinement.
How fragile. How empty.
How nothing, now,
without you.

Dear Readers,

Whenever I hear "we have reached the flying altitude of 30,000+ ft," I'm amazed. Amazed that I'm stationed in a window seat looking down, even though I profess to be afraid of heights. Amazed at the forces and technology that keep us gliding above the clouds. I'm even in awe that flying is my mode of transportation (at times) because when I was growing up, we traveled all distances by car and train.

There's something about being that high. I've been inspired to rest and write while 33,000 ft in the air. But I've also had moments of fright being at such an elevation. Like the time the pilot announced 30 minutes into our flight that we had to make an emergency landing because we were losing hydraulic fluid. We landed safely but during those moments that we glided toward Dulles International Airport unexpectedly, I held my breath and prayed for safety.

But isn't that how life is? Full of moments when we're so high that we're enjoying a different type of air, and others where we feel like we're falling fast and furiously toward a diverted destination. Just like flying, once you actually start to live, you're no longer in control. No matter how hard we try, or how hard I try to write a script for my life, it never follows suit. And for the most part, I'm glad it's that way. Sure, I'm still waiting on some dreams to come true, but here I am, guest editor of *Yellow Arrow Journal*, Vol. IX, No. 1, **ELEVATE**, putting together an issue that will take us higher.

From the poignant cover of **ELEVATE** to the brilliant words that adorn each page, this issue is like flying above the clouds, in a never-ending sky, over terrain that's both foreign and familiar. Work that's about overcoming and accepting where we are. Stories about loss and love. There are poems that allow us to be in the sky while we march on the ground. And creative nonfiction that gives us permission to cry and proclaim that we're not afraid.

I'm so thankful for the fabulous women-identifying writers who chose to share their hearts in this way. It's not easy to write about trauma or death or forgiveness or eating greasy food and still find ways to make the topics soar.

I hope the possibilities of elevating emanate from the pages as fiercely as a plane's engine when it takes off. Every moment etched within this issue symbolizes that we've reached the flying altitude of 30,000+ ft. Please know that it's safe to unbuckle your seatbelt and relax for the remainder of the ride. Trust me, this is one you'll enjoy and that you'll want to take over and over again.

Thank you for flying!

Sincerely,

Jennifer N. Shannon
Guest Editor

P.S. I asked each contributor to answer the following question: *How does your selected piece elevate you and/or your artistry?* (You can find the contributors' responses at the end of this issue.) As I reflect on the question myself, there are three ways that my artistry has been elevated while guest editing **ELEVATE:**

1) As a reader of all the work submitted, I witnessed so much talent and vulnerability that I've been inspired to think differently, take chances, and be more open in my writing.

2) Being "behind the scenes" of putting together a journal issue gave me insights into the reasons one piece makes it into an issue while another doesn't. It was also a great exercise in collaboration with others who had a vested interest in the success of the issue.

3) Finally, being a guest editor gave me the courage to trust my instincts and the confidence to have a vision for how **ELEVATE** should look, feel, and sound. Most importantly, it prepared me to take on this kind of role again in the future. Thank you to Yellow Arrow!

ELEVATE

Anatomy of a Lumpia Girl
Angelica Terso

These days, I'm made of 50% rice and 50% anger.

One might rightfully wonder what I look like. And I guess it would depend on who you ask. If it's my mom or any of my Filipino titas, I'm *chubby*. If it's random strangers, perhaps I'm *big-boned* or *athletic*. It's a lucky thing for me that my family immigrated to America, where people sometimes care about hurting other people's feelings. My best friends would argue that I'm beautiful and perfect, and exotic, and *sexy*. They love me too much.

No matter how I'm described on the outside, everyone would agree that I come with a side of sass and fury.

"For fuck's sake," I groan against a lumpy pillow that's probably a hundred years old.

Mama never likes to throw away anything. Sheets and towels are repurposed as furniture covers and bathroom mats. The filling in old pillows is used to stuff other old pillows. Second-hand stereos, even ones with dangling wires and blown out speakers, are still used to blast cha-cha music at eight o'clock in the morning.

"Really?" I yell out, even though I know they can't hear me over the beat thumping the thin walls.

My alarm won't go off for another 30 minutes, but I get up anyway. Sometimes, I don't know if my parents are really unaware, or if they're purposefully making my mornings miserable so I will finally move out.

I think that both are true.

I guess I don't blame them. I would do the same if my 27-year-old daughter moved back home after her marriage failed, snatching away the promise of them finally being empty nesters.

"How'd you sleep?" Mama asks as she scoops out two big spoonfuls of garlic fried rice onto my plate.

I may be chubby by our culture's standards, but my mother would never deny her child garlic fried rice in the morning. And regular white rice midday. And adobo fried rice at dinner time.

"Good," I shrug through a mouthful of lumpia. Spring rolls aren't typically served in the mornings, but Mama knows they're my favorite.

"Are you ready for today?"

"I guess."

"You have everything in your bag?"

"Yup."

"Do you have to say anything when you get there?"

"I don't fucking know, Mom," I breathe out, dropping my fork and spoon with a loud clang. "It's not like I've ever gotten a divorce before."

I get up from the table with my plate still full, hunger replaced by a brewing storm. Ten years ago, she probably would've slapped me in the face. But 10 years ago, I also wouldn't have dared to say the F-word in front of my parents.

I swear I wasn't always this angry.

I ignore the repeated sounds and notifications that pop up on my phone and switch it to Do Not Disturb. I can already imagine what my friends are texting. "You got this!" "You're a queen, and it's time to pick your crown back up." "There are better days ahead." Or some other bullshit generic quotes they found on Pinterest while on the toilet this morning. Anything to make getting a divorce and starting over sound like a glamorous adventure they wish they were on.

"Traffic ahead," Google says.

"Idiots."

The map shows a car crash close by, delaying my drive by another 17 minutes. Luckily, I left the house early, so I'll still make it on time. Unluckily, the traffic is bumper-to-bumper, cars moving at a snail's pace. So slow that I notice the building to my right, my old high school, its peeling paint visible even from the highway, its two Hs faded so that it reads as oward igh School.

I wonder if the underside of the bleachers still has our initials. I wonder if the last stall in the girls' bathroom next to the gym still has my name and his with hearts all around it.

I never expected to have a boyfriend in high school. I was never anyone's crush. Our school district was majority white, and Asians weren't cool or fetishized just yet (*The Fast and the Furious: Tokyo Drift* wouldn't come out until years later). Plus, I was chubby and quiet. But somehow, a boy from geometry class liked me. It wasn't a prank like I thought it was when he asked for my number and called the same night. And though there were many awkward silences and shy glances as inexperienced teenagers do, there was mutual likeness, and eventually there was love. Years later, we got married.

The driver behind me lays on his horn for 12 whole seconds, and my fingers instinctively curl up, leaving the middle one standing.

"Fuck off, grandpa," I grumble, stepping on the gas pedal, just now noticing that the traffic ahead has cleared.

His car is the first thing I notice when I pull into the parking lot. It's hard to miss with all its theatrical extras. Tinted windows, big exhaust, and high spoilers. Even while parked, the car is annoyingly loud.

"I'm here for my divorce hearing," I say to the receptionist, well aware that *he's* in the corner reading a magazine.

I pick one up, too, and sit on a chair when I'm asked to wait. It's a *Women's Health Magazine* that has Vanessa Hudgens showing off her flat stomach on the cover.

He never told me who the other woman was. I never asked. But for months, my imagination was in overdrive. She's probably blonde, him having gotten sick of my jet black hair. Or maybe she's a redhead, something new and exciting. Or perhaps she has an edgy, short bob that's half shaved on the side. Anyway, the hair doesn't matter. I just always imagined her with a flat stomach like Vanessa Hudgens.

When we finally enter the small conference room, the judge in front of us is old and has to lick his fingers every time he turns a page. "Are these dates correct?"

"Yes."

We sit across from each other at a long rectangular table, stacks of papers between us. It feels like we're merely colleagues from different departments forced to have a meeting that could've been an email. I catch him eyeing the new tattoo on my forearm, seeing it for the first time. I can tell he doesn't like it.

"Well, that's that," the judge says. "I just need you both to sign and date here."

I release the breath I didn't know I was holding.

Well, that's that.

"Take it easy," *he* says when we leave the judge's stuffy office. I almost scoff. How is starting over supposed to be easy?

"Take care," I say. I don't know why I said that.

I don't start my car, but I turn the ringer on my phone back on and scroll past several messages. I'm not ready to be cheered up by my friends just yet, but I do click on one thread.

"I'm thinking of you this morning. In fact, I'm thinking of you always. You can cry if you want to. It's a sad day. - Mama."

And for the first time in years, I do what my mother says.

I wrap my arms around my body, slightly rocking back and forth as my vision blurs. I cry for the home we dreamt about together, the one with the big backyard and white fence. I cry for the kids we were planning to have, one boy and one girl. I cry for our nonexistent future, growing old together on rocking chairs on a wrap-around porch. I cry for myself, for being comfortable, for daring to be hopeful. For still missing me after everything.

I stay in the parking lot until the workers who left for lunch get back. Until my body feels tired and the tightness in my chest goes away. And when my stomach begins to rumble, I finally turn the key.

No one talks to me when I walk into the house. Papa pretends to trim his indoor plants, and Mama doesn't mention my puffy eyes.

"I'm going to go take a nap," I announce.

"Take these. They're freshly cooked," Mama says, handing me a bowl of lumpia.

"Thanks, Ma." I hold her gaze for a moment longer. We're not sentimental in this family, but I hope she knows I mean thank you for the other thing, too.

I sit on my childhood bed. There are colorful stickers I had stuck on the walls of my room when I was in high school, random shapes arranged together to form big and small waves. He and I used to sit here after school, craning our necks as we stared at the outlines surrounding us, fantasizing and wishing we were somewhere warmer with our toes buried in the sand.

Instead of letting my body collapse on the bed like it begs to, I peel the stickers off, one by one, until the walls are bare, save for the sticky residue. Tomorrow I'm going to take a wet, soapy sponge and scrub them clean.

I decide to sit on the floor and wipe my face with a wet cloth. And then I eat the lumpia, catching the crumbs with one hand. I let my shoulders fall, my body relax, and my stomach loosen.

I tilt my head to the side in wonder. Ever since I can remember, my body's first instinct is to always suck my stomach in. How freeing it feels not to do that. And how powerful. And how *beautiful*.

I cry again.

Right now, I'm made of 50% lumpia and 100% grateful.

I know I'm 150% terrible at math.

To Forgive You
Annabelle Taghinia

It took most of a year, a sunny day, and a really nice warm shower
for me to forgive you. The sunlight leaked through the window
and refracted in the steam rising from the water, splayed across
the tile in its winding geometric patterns, and I pressed my hands
with their dry cracking exterior against the shape and watched
the color flit across my parched skin and realized there was no
point in holding on, and remembered that you're still growing, too,
and remembered that youth gives us unbalanced emotions and
underdeveloped bodies and wounds that will close and scar but
never fade, and remembered that you treated me with kindness and
gave me your gloves when I left mine at home, and remembered
that I forget the way you look but only in the way that every time I
picture your face your nose is a different shape and your cheeks
fuller or thinner than they really are, your eyebrows waxing and
waning with the trajectory of your cosmetic appointments, and as
I stood there, vulnerable and alone, warm and clean, I washed you
off me and down the drain along with all the other things it
had come time for me to shed, and every winter my hands crack
under the cool air and constant handwashing I inherited from my
parents and even though they eventually bleed, you are not here to
see it anymore. It took most of a year, a sunny day, and a shower,
but I remembered that the world turns on.

malea
Michele Evans

[ma-lee-ah] n. a Greek peninsula and a flowering plant,
the Latin root mal means bad or evil

i was hopeless, running away from home and him and hurt
when a lush overgrown island of lotus blossoms welcomed me

to a new dawn, after the ninth day the gods finally showed favor,
and i washed ashore, rescued by natives who would rehab me

far beyond the waves, my addiction took residence
with other diseased, until doctors prescribed me

daily sunray shots eventually fading the rope
bracelets i wore where he once tattooed me,

with swallowed pills and rainwater i washed down
murky memories from pasts that punched me

hardest during nights' silences when all patients
become prisoners to tremors, those that reminded me

of being enclosed, tied up, homebound in a darkened pod,
exposed only to brief flickers of sky when he fed me

platefuls of side effects: windowless yellowed eyes,
slowed heartbeats, numb limbs supporting a weakened me,

on my knees, hands clasped shedding grief's residue,
an all you can eat buffet of worry, behind me

so i rebelled and rebloomed, rose to the surface,
floating, feeling both resurrected and rapturous,

my petals showy, reviving and thriving
in rich loam, i, thick stemmed, honey skinned,

at last hopeful, learned how to forgive . . . me.

Rising to the Occasion
Sara Palmer

Fall, 2023: An Easy Hike

My younger son, always the optimist, says this will be an easy
hike, a walk on naked ski slopes in the Taconic Mountains before
the season's first snowfall. Autumn leaves blaze fire orange, a few
scattered pawpaws banana yellow. We set out on clear paths, wide
as roads, the children running ahead. "Easy, easy," I say to my
heart, its pounding like a waterfall, as the slope rises straight up
the mountainside, alarmingly steep. One foot, then the other. I
cheer myself on silently, don't say a word. I picture the vast view
of mountains and valleys that will be my prize when we reach the
summit, imagine how many have struggled up mountains before
me, to find their vistas, to worship their gods, to test their mettle.
"Failure is impossible," said Susan B. Anthony. The quote pops into
my mind and sticks, a mantra for the road ahead of me. Soon my
heart slows, my bones slide easily in their sockets, my breath takes
back its usual rhythms. Up, up I go, into the dense beauty of infinite
elevations.

"Thank you," I say to my son, "for choosing an easy hike."

Winter, 2024: Stepping It Up

On January 1st, the day after my 68th birthday, my older son and I
went hiking in the mountains near Los Angeles. He didn't tell me
how many miles we'd walk, how long it would take, or how hard it
would be, and I didn't ask. "Your reward for making it to the top,"
he tells me as we leave the car at the trailhead, "will be me revealing
the total elevation." Game on.

We set out late in the day, the afternoon light already fading. The
trail is not exceptionally steep but climbs steadily uphill. I feel my

heart rate increasing, my leg muscles whining. At each turn of the road, I wonder if we should quit and head back down. But a brand new 68th birthday voice in my head is telling me, "Step it up while you still can." I listen and keep climbing.

When we reach the top, the sun is dipping low behind the city, and a golden swath of light shimmers on the Pacific Ocean, far in the distance. I feel exhilarated, brave, energized. I am awestruck by the vista before me, but equally by my own powers of healing after the full stop terror of a heart attack three years ago. Untold hours pushing myself to the max in cardiac rehab and, later, in the gym have paid off, and here I am, hiking up a mountain. I am happy to be alive, to embrace the future with its risks, surprises, and possibilities for joy.

The way down is fast and easy. The sun has set and it's cold. I put my hands in my pockets while my son lights the road ahead with his cell phone flashlight. We are both elated with a case of runner's high, and the lights twinkling on in the valley below look super bright and trippy. When we reach the residential neighborhood at the foot of the trail, multicolored Christmas lights are on in front of many houses. "Don't you just love those lights?" my son says, grinning like a kid. He doesn't say he's proud of me or amazed that I made it. I'm the one who can't resist stating the obvious: "Pretty good for an old lady, huh?" Clearly, he trusts in my powers—I've mothered him, after all. He knew I could do it. Still, the next day, he checks in with me: "So, Mom, how are you feeling today after that hike?" Surprisingly, I feel great, and I tell him so. "Glad to hear it," he says, "cause my legs kinda hurt."

Elevation revealed: 1,600 ft.

Webb Surfing
Mary Moreno

(After viewing NASA's deep space images from the James Webb telescope)

Back before there was a breath,
  beyond the boundaries of time,
    sits this glimpse of a beginning.

Awash in a sea of starlight
  and vast splashes of color,
    denser than Van Gogh's dreams.

The cosmos shifted and shaped and sang us into being.
  Born of stars we are,
    birthed by the light of eternity.

pilot
Carter Lappin

when she was 10 she snuck a book on airplanes out of the library
under her puffy purple coat. at home, she went out her brother's
window and climbed onto the roof to read it. she turned
through the pages with a scholarly sort of reverence. when they
came to find her she lay flat on her back on the hot tile so they
couldn't see her as they circled like carrion birds down below. she
squinted, eyes tearing, up at the blue sky and the yellow sun. far
off, an airplane soared. she pretended she was up there with it, and,
when she closed her eyes, she could almost hear the beautiful
screaming of the engines, drowning out all noise that came from
beneath. why would an airplane ever land, she wondered, when
there was all that sky?

*Thank you to the woman leaning out her window
and drumming as we marched for Roe in 2022*
Daisy Bassen

You made me look around and then up.
There I saw you through the iron lacework
Of the maple's first leaves

                like Murillo's
Two Women at a Window and you both,
The younger one watching, the older holding
Back the shutter, obscured, taking in

                the livid world
At a necessary distance and you beat the drum
Hard, in time with the chant we answered,
We tried to find a rhythm using

                our own hearts,
Halting until we heard you and then we shouted
Now and **power** and ***freedom***! You reminded
Me there can be a visceral joy

                in striking skin,
There can be a dark-eyed woman above in a window
With her drum when you are only looking ahead,
Trying to be loud. You can be given

                what you need.

NAIF CAFE,
brooklyn baggett

5,827 miles from America
& the Deep South moves
into the table behind me:
two drawling cis women.
they are *old & full of wisdom*, they say.

Greek patrons
speak in communal voices;
chain smoke
while their country burns.

they talk of organized citizens
dousing wildfires with tiny pails,
of carrying supplies—water, food, masks—
into impossibility. they solve
for the displaced dogs & cats—
who might foster them?
they speak like people
5,000 years old.

> *how much is that worth?*
> *how. much. is. that. worth?* she presses—
> with her poor poor person smile.
> *how much is*
> *that one little coin, sugar?*
> *.5 euro*, the server responds.
> *thank you, shug*—turns back to her conversation.

i waste food & feel ashamed;
i write this poem in anger.
i make this moment
about me.

i am ashamed i speak one language,
like the previous night
at ΚΑΦΑ Bar, sitting with the owner, George,
an endless procession of queer magic.
i meet someone from Berlin, from Tehran.
they speak three languages.
Ali shows me family photos,
leans in like we're old friends.
he's a translator for refugees.
he's an anarchist,
not a persona.
he is angry—
but only at structures.
he scrolls through instagram
me: *looking at beautiful people?*
Ali: *we are all beautiful people.*

i long to be a local.
i want to be Greek & know other languages.
to clean my plate &
know the real value of .5 euro,
to think about fostering dogs.
i want to be Iranian & bring the sun to new people.
i want to be angry at systems, not people
& think to say things like:
this is my sister. isn't she beautiful?

Baptism
Shieva Salehnia

The fountain in the middle of Washington Square Park has not
always been there, just as I have not always been here,
standing next to it.

In the middle of the park, I climb inside the edge of the fountain's lips.
I lean back against them, the cool slick stone. The bubbling center spray
spurts, streams, arcs, rushing into the filthy city sky; plumes so
massive, they summon the smell of the ocean.

The water washes away the weight of people's attention,
the unrelenting mess of the city disappears off my ankles, swollen
and ashen from the heat and sticky grime of each sidewalk
I pressed my soul against to get here.

100 years ago, the star magnolias didn't grow on the trees
at the park's edge. But now the flower beds bloom
with bluebells and red and yellow lipped tulips.

We are transplants, the flowers, the fountain, and I. Yet,
we are each perfect manifestations here.
Nature never gives up.
I remind myself I am part of nature.
We never give up.

Migraine
Jordan Eve Morral

I know a place where construction men hammer away at nails all day. A place where an emerging indie rock band practices their song list. A place where elementary kids play a giant game of duck, duck, goose. It is as busy as an airport over the holidays; everyone is obstreperous. And all of this takes place in one large, open room. (The echo—due to the room's vastness—only adds to the noise.)

I go there every other week or so. Sometimes construction is paused. Other times the band isn't playing. But every time, without fail, the place is in utter chaos.

I am there right now. I don't know how I got there, though. I was reading a book under a tree and the next thing I knew, I was in the center of the pandemonium. How long ago was that? Have I only been here for a few minutes? It feels like much longer.

The band is practicing a new number, something with a lot of drums. Really, it would be quite good if it weren't for the sound of children screaming in the background. I like the song's rhythm, but I can't appreciate it, not now.

The construction guys are at their usual post, hammering and sawing away but making no visible progress. I often wonder why they are here; do they have something to accomplish, or are they simply enjoying the monotony of their work?

And there goes a line of people singing something that sounds like, "cha-cha cha-cha cha-cha." That's a new addition. They dance their way around the circle of duck, duck, goose players. Except, upon closer inspection, I see that the game is in complete disarray. Now, the once organized circle of players looks more like a game of tag where everyone is "it."

My eyes search for a door (it's time to leave), but I see none. No windows, no stairs—nothing. I have no means of escape. But I already knew that. (I've been here before, remember?) I just had to make sure.

I don't want to join in on the madness; I'm afraid I will lose my faculties, spiral toward insanity, and be forever stuck in this nightmare. So instead, in the center of the chaos, I lay down. The cement floor is uncomfortable, but I curl up in a ball with my hands under my head. My makeshift pillow.

With thoughts that are no longer coherent, I am conscious of only one thing: I have become a passive creature at the mercy of sadistic strangers. They lay not a hand on me but are fueled by my growing discomfort, like a machine that moves faster when oiled. I must try my very best to deprive them of that satisfaction, for I am capable of nothing else.

As the mayhem continues around me, I lay and wish for sleep to come.

This is a poem about birth trauma
Bethany Tap

It is talking about a thing without talking about it.

It is circling the edges   of a widening gyre

moving against   the wind   ripping   facts apart

and scattering   truth   like   you'd blow seeds

off a dandelion   stem   then   closing your eyes and

wishing   for the   pieces   to spin   back together

to form   a new   picture or   perspective   to morph   the past into

something   palatable   something   you can   look at   without

retching   without   hating   yourself   without   guilt (guilt

is the   reason   you   laugh   off   the word

trauma—   trauma   implies   bad   things   but you're

fine,   remember?   And baby?   Baby is   fine   fine fine fine.

Everyone   is fine.   Remember?)   It is easier   to forget than

to talk about it   (don't talk about it).   It is easier to write a poem   or a story about

the thing that happened   to someone else   not you, not yours   it wasn't you who

failed, it wasn't you who   couldn't do it,   it wasn't your sliced open   (unfit) uterus.

I can rewrite this, repaint this, reframe this, so that it's not me. It was never me.

This is not my story   my poem. This is someone else's.

I'm just the writer.

Small
Sarah Piper

I fell sick, first,
and then illness made me small
and shed notes from my voice
and ate up my cells like puny chickens,
and nothing came in the mail for years,
and no task needed doing, except all of living—
just keep living.

I unplugged the television
and gave away all my clothes
and taped photos to the insides of windows
until the earth drank up the winter sky
and I could open them wide and fresh
to hear the birds scratch and shuffle the ground for food.

I learned to wait in the line of life.

And I remembered how easy it is to learn, small,
when every scouting ant is that teacher
with a raised eyebrow, waiting on me
to ease into a world still too new
and too big for knowing—
each day its own line through the tall grass;

and so, I stopped pretending
to know at all,
anything,
except that love is not silly
and can be slathered on a day like peanut butter,
and silly isn't silly,
and no small thing is ever small:

even sitting like a dot on the edge of a gently rotating day

could almost put me in the sky.

Girl on the Edge
Rebecca D. Martin

I'm on the edge of the photograph, which feels all too familiar. Call it what you will: being off-screen, fading into the background, a quiet apology for my existence. Even now, I am uncomfortable with that young version of myself in the picture. I am tempted to look away, resisting my own gaze.

Forty-six years old, I sit at my desk in my house, a sensory haven. Every visual, aural, and olfactory need is accounted for so I can feel quiet and safe—everything I didn't know I needed from my childhood environment. I look at the photograph of myself on my computer screen. I'm standing in my family's pineapple-decorated kitchen. I had turned 16 that very day, and I, the girl in the right hand corner, slip as far off-screen as possible. I reach for her, but no. You do not yet know how to love me, she says. She'll hide herself in me 'til the time is right.

It is late in the evening in the photograph because she has just been to an Indigo Girls concert at the Fox Theater in downtown Atlanta. The three friends who celebrated her birthday with her are intentionally arranged in the shirts they bought at intermission: the shirt with two white hands holding a string of beads in a shape like a smile, the shirt with the "Rites of Passage Tour" image, and the shirt with a photo of Emily and Amy, from the band. I, the girl in the corner of the photograph, am also wearing the hands shirt. Those big white hands and the bead-string smile make a haunting face that is a little unsettling and definitely interesting.

Look how happy those young women are—and how tired. The Indigo Girls show had been incredible, and none of them minded the nosebleed seats. They sang along the whole time. *Rites of Passage* might have been the band's most singable album. It's certainly the one to which I still know all the harmonies, musical muscle memory kicking in with gusto: "Three Hits," "Virginia

Woolf," and that echoing promise down the years, "Love Will Come to You."

Funny what the girl on the end will remember years later, though. In the midnight recap, bundled in sleeping bags, "Did you hear the note they ended on in 'Closer to Fine'?" asks the friend in the Amy/Emily shirt, disbelieving. "Yeah!" agrees my friend in the "Rites of Passage Tour" shirt. "It was way off." They cringe and laugh together. The girl on the edge hadn't noticed the wrong notes at all. Lying quiet in her sleeping bag, she tried to pretend in front of all of them that there wasn't something wrong about the way she perceived the world.

The next morning, the three friends would go home. And that afternoon, the girl on the edge will find herself overwhelmed by the influx of noise and exhaustion and probably the inordinate amounts of Dr. Pepper or Mountain Dew, not to mention birthday cake. Her mind will buzz, a hot confusion, and for some reason, she will hold a bag of Skittles, her favorite candy. It wasn't one of those little skinny packs that deliver a scant 12 or 15 shiny round rainbow fruit confections in the hand, but large enough that when she's standing in the very center of the kitchen and has had enough—I mean enough—of the massive, roiling thoughts and feelings that can't settle or jive, she cast the bag to the floor so violently that the large number of candies skittered, bounced, and rolled across the beige linoleum. Thousands of rainbow shards finding corners to land in, spinning like tops as the inexplicable rage ran out of her body and into the ether and settled, instead, into embarrassment. From the table in the bay window, her younger brother and his friend would gaze at her, wide-eyed.

The girl on the edge will be embarrassed—yes, I see her nodding her head in the photograph to affirm—and ashamed. She knows so little about herself, and almost all the information is wrong. For instance, she won't know to call this a meltdown. She doesn't know how necessary meltdowns are or how understandably autistic. Nothing to feel guilty or wrong about. She doesn't know

that all the sights and sounds and social efforts of the night before
added up to a very particular kind of burnout, or that it's okay to
hear the notes differently, or that the songs themselves were lifting
her, holding her in a safe space amid the overstimulation. She
won't know she's autistic for 29 more years, and she will carry the
discomfort of this episode, wondering why no one asked, "Why
did you do that?" or, "What's going on here?" or, "Are you okay?"
Her mother will quietly sweep up the candies and slide them into
the trash while the girl sits on the floor with her back against the
cabinets and cries.

The night before, after the concert, that pineapple wallpaper
running an early 90s backdrop to the four smiling young women,
she was happy. The songs ran and ran through her head in the
intensive way they do after a live show with promises that love will
come, dancing our way toward brighter places, with messages sent
to the soul that say, "You're okay."

It has only been a few years since I've understood how things
can be good and bad at the same time, and how not everything has
a simple answer, but how sometimes it does, and how the answer is
nothing to be ashamed of. The answer, in a sense, puts the shame
to shame. It kills it, just as the love comes in. I hold forward this
message to the girl on the edge of the picture, and I tell her it's
time; she can stop hiding herself. I ask if she's ready to talk about
autism—to talk about being different, and how different is okay.
She might not be ready to talk yet, but she starts humming, and it's
something about being closer to fine, and the music lifts me now as
it always has, and I join in.

Tap Dancing in Stop & Shop
Robin Dellabough

My son's daughter spends the weekend we have to
stock up on gluten-free dairy-free soy-free food

she's eight already knows which brand
of bread or pasta or oat milk she likes best

she feeds her heavy mama and herself
says she's fine with no hugs and okay with her father

disappearing for years she thinks he's in a hospital
getting better but there's no cure for his brand of demons

she skips down the aisles filled with bright boxes
of cookies crackers she can't eat uncomplaining

in the middle of the store her tight brown coils
bounce as she shows me a tap dance routine

I can't stop beaming she's learned this
one thing she didn't have to learn

Escapee
Glenis Moore

Scrambling over the fence,

like a prison absconder,

its stems entwined and knotted

with rambling roses and ivy,

the squash plant flowered and fruited

high above our neighbour's garden.

A bright, burnished lantern glowing

gloriously amidst the branches.

Proof positive, for all to see,

of the ripe goodness entombed

in our old, deserted compost heap.

On the mats
Morgan Sheehan

The first gym I walked into was in South Deerfield, just over seven miles from my house in western Massachusetts. I hadn't gotten a recommendation so much as told it was there. Krav Maga. Developed for the Israeli Defense Force. The Internet told me this was "real" self-defense. Perhaps the size of the gym should have given me pause, but I had no experience with martial arts, "real" or otherwise.

The gym was small; it was once a narrow shop. Benches faced a slightly raised platform; I took a seat. A tall, fit young man was coaching a one-on-one session with an older man. This was about fear. Would he be able to protect himself? What if they tried to take his wallet? What if they had a knife? A gun? The scenarios played out behind the older man's eyes, making his feet heavy and his hands slow.

Ever so carefully, the instructor attacked with a bright blue, plastic knife. All I could think was, *who does he think is going to knife him in South Deerfield*? Population 2,000. You're more likely to be hit with an errant potato.

The private session ended with a flurry of questions from the older man and repeated reassurance from the coach that they would go over more the next time. The older man walked out, shoulders hunched forward. The young coach disappeared into the back, and the regulars entered the gym for class. That's why I was there. My heart rate picked up a notch.

The gym owners, two men in their 40s, a little older than me with impressively expansive stomachs, had just returned from a Krav Maga seminar. Their excitement filled the narrow space; they had learned so much. Had so much to share. This was all stuff that worked "on the street." They said that a lot. Especially when holding the bright blue plastic knife.

I should have walked out then.

There were six men, two younger and four middle aged. And two women, one young and one my age. Both small and birdlike.

"You're the trial?" one of the gym owners asked. Sometimes over email people think I'm a man; my name could go either way. They usually don't think that in person. The other looked at me and corrected, "She's here to OBSERVE the class," downgrading me on sight. I had signed up for a trial but already knew I wasn't going to join. Nobody in this gym was going to give me what I wanted, which was, perhaps absurdly, what it felt like to fight.

"We get a lot of people like you."

"Oh?" I replied. A lot of writers looking for information about full contact combat sports because of a story? I didn't say that.

He continued talking, this time bringing his voice down low to give the impression of privacy in the tiny room. "A lot of SA victims come here. Don't worry, you won't have to be afraid anymore," he said, with a reassuring nod. "Not after this."

Victims was the word that stood out to me; I had to roll SA over in my mind for a second. When I looked back at the mat, everyone was staring at me. They thought I had been assaulted. That I was afraid. That I needed this so I would feel safe again.

The older of the two women joined me on the benches, sitting in the row in front of me. The cast on her arm presumably keeping her off the mats.

Turning around, she looked unblinking into my eyes. "It's scary at first, but you'll get better." Her fingers curled, white knuckled, over the back of the bench. She meant, "get better after the assault." But I wasn't angry at her. She was sharing how it was for her, her whole body still rigid with hyperawareness.

I watched the class for 30 minutes, fascinated and angrier every second that ticked by. They had no balance. No spatial awareness. The man who partnered with the younger woman was never corrected by the coaches even though he almost injured her at every repetition.

I left having never stepped on the mat. Shaking off their assumptions about me at the door.

It took me another week to try again. I didn't want another gym to think I was a victim.

Here's the thing. I have been assaulted. Lots of women have. But it doesn't define me. I didn't need a gym so I wouldn't be afraid anymore. That's not what I was looking for and having them assume that about me made my skin crawl.

The second gym was bigger. There were more people. More women. More Eminem blasting over the speakers. Members wore starchy white uniforms that made me think "martial arts" but in a generic way. Brazilian jiu-jitsu. I didn't know what it was; I hadn't looked it up like I had Krav Maga.

They said to wear comfortable clothing. I did. They gave me a gi that smelled like every single pubescent teen boy had sweat in it before me. I put it on anyway. My own special, smelly pair of uncomfortable fight pajamas. They said to join everybody on the mats. I did. Already everything felt different. Nobody asked me if I was there because I was afraid. Fear didn't have a place in the room.

I've never been in bad shape. I've always been strong for my size. I like doing things, and I don't like sitting still. I entered the gym humorously overconfident. After the warmups, I was sweaty and breathing hard. Everyone else knew what to do, how to move. No one else was even flushed in the cheeks.

The coach, a smaller guy who was quick to smile, turned to a giant with a brown belt and said, "Teach her a throw, a submission, and a pass." People around us joked with each other, smiling easily with a hand on the shoulder of the person next to them as they started their lessons.

"You're going to throw me," my interim coach said. His voice was so deep I could barely hear him over the frantic Puerto Rican rap. I laughed at him. He had a shaved head, no smile. Big empty earlobes where double zero gauges usually go. He was 6'5" and all muscle. He had a hundred pounds on me.

He didn't laugh back.

His name was Peter, though the other folks called him Voltron. I didn't know he was a literal world champion in jiu-jitsu. After five minutes of coaching from Peter, I had his weight on my hip, ready to finish the throw. All 230 pounds of him. It was frankly exhilarating.

The submission was weirder. Peter lay on the mat on his back and said, "Okay, get on." So I did that, too, sitting on his stomach, my knees on either side of his hips, chest to chest. My ear to his bulbous, scarred one.

After clearing my hair out of his face he said, "Jiu-jitsu is close. We all forget that it's weird. It was weird for us, too, when we started. If you're worried about it, just know that it's not weird to me. I do this all the time."

And then he showed me how to choke him. I was hooked.

The six months I gave myself to learn about combat sports turned into more than five years. I can't imagine leaving. What is it that hooked me so deeply? The competition? The joy and intimacy of fighting physically? The almost instant closeness of a team? The fact that I, now 44, can beat a younger man twice my size and that one of my coaches, a woman 20 pounds lighter than me, can beat me? All of that. More, I'm sure.

In the gym, I'm stripped down to an essence. Bones and muscles. That's why you'll find me on the mats six days a week. Easy with my own smile. Walking new people through their first weird days. Fearless.

An Extenuation of Thanks
Samantha Liana Williams

Smelling of Crisco,
of pizza puffs & Harold's chicken.
The grease slick against your teeth when
you slide your tongue across them.

Fried dough is what you brave
the deadliest weekend for, in a
jean skirt, tank top & clean white shoes.
It is a three-block walk from the closest bus stop.

You wade through people on both sides,
find the smallest booth without a loud sign.
Just two people; one taking orders the other
a mannequin with tongs.

The styrofoam plate they hand you
a backdrop against weaving.
The plastic fork you won't use,
even the licking of fingers, a sigh.
You feel fancy, tell them to add
whipped cream and strawberries
heavy in their own syrup.

Keri Hilson is on stage two
as you rub oil against your temples.
You wonder if you're going to heaven,
you hope heaven is really Chicago.
Hope that river of gold is a river
of mild sauce.

That this deep coating of powdered sugar,
of Crisco, this lubricant is the thing that takes you.

If Barbie Were My Daughter
Jennifer Martinelli Eyre

If Barbie were my daughter,
I'd take her out to lunch.
Somewhere nice. We wouldn't need
cloth napkins and dress codes.
Tabletop vases with sunflowers would do just fine.
We'd tuck into a corner booth,
plucking our afternoon and cheese fries away
like wildflower petals.
We'd be weightless and full.

We'd sip soda from thick, plastic cups,
letting the fizz tickle the tips of our bumpy noses.
Each bump a reminder of the
knots of our journey. The years of jagged hills,
the leveled valleys that brought us to our lowest, our highest.
Brought us to this booth,
unsliced.

Our hair would be swept up in buns and ponytails.
Undone but done. Silver roots
would catch the sunlight
peeking through restaurant blinds.
We let our hair grow and grow
because it's our roots that tell us who we are,
who we've been.

We'd shovel spoonfuls of chocolate mousse
into our unpainted mouths,
savoring the sweetness
of the words that we share.
Feeding one another the permission,
the sweet courage
to be who we are.
Who we are.
Who we are.

Bellies and souls full,
I'd pay our check and hug her goodbye,
squeezing her until I feel the beat of her heart
pump in sync with mine.
Before we part ways,
I'd tell her I'll see her tomorrow.
Same time.
Same place.
Same booth.
Because if Barbie were my daughter,
lunch with her would forever be
my treat.

Curious Customs of the Dancers of D.C.
Jean Janicke

All this to make a flower out of ostrich feathers.

A ten-year-old tube of Viva Glam lipstick, angled

tip worn from a point to a thumbnail, advertised

"an outspoken red" so smiles reach the back row.

Each piece of the costume laid out last night

like a nomad's blanket unrolled at the souk,

paint patterns mimic silver stitched in scarves,

sequins wink up high slits and drip down hips,

fuchsia silk flutters from a sealed plastic cocoon.

Drink a gallon of water, sing your grandmother's gospel,

bear the weight of your skirts before we hold hands

in dark wings. Fellow dancers lead Twiggy and I

to the marks we can't see in the blackout. A child

in the audience whispers, "it's time for the big finale."

Repast
Susan Shea

You are talking about aging
as though you believe you are down
to the last crumbs on your plate
eating around the bones, letting them

whisper sad songs with your name
limping through them

well I say stop it now, get a hold
of yourself, get up, and come with me
to the buffet table where we can still
wiggle with the jello, smile with the
care bears sitting on the cupcakes, and
taste every single second of this day

and if one of us trips on the way back
to our seated places, we will hold each
other up and start singing a song
about fearless prophets who speak of
marvels, out loud, so all the timid
temporary guests in line
can watch us fill our cups

Lullaby as Lament
Melanie Weldon-Soiset

I sing of loss.
I sing of weeds, and pests.
I sing of night.
I sing of day, then night—the same.

I sing of the wet dog
right before he shimmies.

I sing of the sled, tilting
on the crest of a hill.

Mercy! Do moths eat
their own linen wings?

I sing of dandelion
fluff—acrobatics.

I sing   loss.
  sing   weeds,
        night
        day, then

          the wet dog
             shimmies.

I   tilt
on the crest

Mercy!   moths eat

        dandelion
fluff—acrobatics.

I sing
I sing
I sing

Your Daddy Comes Back as a Monarch
Ann Weil

Some days there is so much noise,
    I about lose my mind.
    Only the soil is mute.

There, I bury my hands deep in the loam,
    raising up bush beans and heirlooms
    like I raised you kids so long ago.

On my knees I lift the weeds,
    shed my worldly vows to men.
    I like to imagine your father

as a winged creature in the next life,
    unburdened by human struggle.
    We could be lighter, together.

Dusk arrives in its lilac robes,
    but I am here for the dirt.
    I promise myself to this patch of earth,

to its kale, cucumbers, and marigolds,
    to love, honor, cherish as long
    as we all shall live. And when

it is my turn to die, scatter me
    in the milkweed bed,
so I may once more see your father.

Reunion
Ellen Blum Barish

The Girl, now a Woman, was searching for her reading glasses when she found me behind a row of books and tennis trophies at her father's house where she left me decades ago. I had waited so long to see her again, weary but patient in spite of the many miles and moves between us, hoping that on one of her hometown visits she would rediscover me at the back of the crowded shelf. When she reached for me and I was back in her touch, I was whole again, but I felt her familiar ache, the pain she had pressed into me when she brought me to life.

Twenty years before, when she was 12, there had been a terrible car accident on her ride home from school. A Mack truck collided into the station wagon her friend's mother was driving that day. The impact knocked her face against the seatback, the front tooth from her mouth, and the voice from her throat. Worse was the hush afterward; there were no comforting words or tender hugs from her parents. The silencing had been to body and soul.

Some years later, in a high school art class, I was placed before her as a formless lump of clay, and her small hands and fingers found the strength to express what her vocal cords couldn't. She molded me into a mirror of herself: a prepubescent nude sitting on her knees. Since then, I've carried the weight of her pain, even after she left me on that shelf as I waited patiently, hoping for our reunion.

Once back home from her father's house, she unwrapped me from two rolled up T-shirts and set me gently on her dresser. Our eyes locked, her hand lingered, and she picked me up and brought me closer.

She turned me around, taking me in as one takes in an artifact, noting the indents of my eyes, the suggestion of my ears, the cliff of my cheeks, the slope of my nose. But then her gaze lowered, and she stiffened; light splintered her eyes as she took in the bottom half of my face, which she had kneaded smooth. There were no lips or teeth, just a flat surface of solidified silence. I was a message delivered in clay, a vessel for her voice, once fired shut, cracked open and brought into the light.

begin again
Tramaine Suubi

hold your body, cradle yourself in your own arms. as you hug every
fragment, study each one. hold them to the light. then bind them
together with gold. may the scars glitter & fill you with wonder like
the stars above

examine the landscape of your body. become familiar with the
scenery. stand before a large mirror. strip. as you peel each layer,
gently run your hands over your skin, your hair, your nails. as the
last thread floats off your body, look up at the mirror & drink in the
vision before you. do a little dance & marvel at how the landscape
shifts

cleanse the rubble of the past from your body. do so patiently as the
toxins, the dead skin, the excess pool at your feet, give thanks for
seasons & develop an appreciation for cycles. bathe in the beauty
of forgiveness & be washed in grace. rinse & repeat as needed

drink up. you have emptied yourself to start over. replenish your
body. you are made of mostly water, so fill yourself with mostly
water. conjure lavish blends. learn to make your drinks from
scratch. harvest your own ingredients if you can. embrace a lifestyle
of fresh-squeezed & home-brewed. toast to yourself as you master
moderation

savor your daily bread. fill your body with the fresh & colorful,
sample the cuisines of all cultures. relish every bite & sensation,
feast on the flavors offered by our tender earth. plant some by the
window & blend your own in the kitchen. teach your body to crave
homemade goodness. cultivate an intimate relationship with food

rise. seek out your body's happy place. it may be the woods or the
water, the studio or the slopes. find your space & become familiar
with it. gather up your energy & open your body. move with
intentionality. exchange tight for loose. fine-tune your technique
& push for daily effort. experience the miracle of the physical. your
body is a force of nature, harness that power

rest. the creator created a day just for rest, but creation needs it
every day. your body is not infinite. treat it as such. listen to the
warning bells & look out for the red flags. study your circadian
rhythms & protect your sleep cycle. understand that you also need
to rest while you are awake. remember that being idle is not
the same as being rested

become an alchemist. eden may be hidden but the majik remains,
find her remnants in the raw, unrefined, organic, whole. extract
carefully. wrap your skin in heavenly scents. nourish your hair with
pure oils. strengthen your nails with rich vitamins

unroll your hippocampus. decode & deconstruct the memories as
they unfold. embrace the crest of feeling, the trough of emotion,
preserve the fingerprints left on your heart. breathe, beloved. accept
that healing is not linear. for now, you are still here

Over the Rainbow
Rachel R. Baum

My father played Over the Rainbow
on his saxophone until he couldn't,
so he whistled it instead.

The tune seemed to live in his throat, as though
some invisible pressure compelled him, one way
or another, to release it from between his pursed lips.

His whistled version of the song had a jazz tempo
like Ella and Billie, Sarah Vaughn and Eva Cassidy,
he reshaped it into a sunset, familiar and beautiful.

Its cadence was languid, the bridge longer and higher,
its refrain as fluid as a coat of paint, tinting the air
a deep, resonant blue.

He chased the melody behind the moon,
beyond the stars, wrapping wistful melancholy
into notes that saddened and soared.

My mother signed off from all our phone
conversations by saying, "Dad sends his love,"
words he himself had never spoken.

When he whistled Over the Rainbow, I thought of it
as his gift that warmed the sky, gave it summer,
and tucked its colors into every goodbye.

Obituary
Elizabeth Hill

After C.D. Wright

I often chewed ice at night. My hands
were veined and my nails painted pink. I did not write poems.
I was always looking for a newspaper article on
how to choose the right color of azaleas. If I were still in Exeter
and you were still there, too, we would meet at Swazy Parkway and
watch the water run. We would have a grand time. Watching, eyes soft.
Do not mourn me or cry. I'm looking for a tennis court which hosts
heavenly hosts like me and does not hog the ball.
I know people who have died alone; take Matthew Perry. I want
to taunt the God who thinks he (or she) took me away from you.
You know, if I had stepped on a bathroom scale on Venus, I would
have weighed 122.85 pounds. But I am leaving Venus now, headed
God knows where. The dirt is dark, deep, and clammy. Unlike the others,
I'm not one to predict worms. I saw Peggy Fleming win gold.
I was nine and brave when Hitler took his life. If I had been
wiser, I would have married my husband's brother, who ran
the auto repair on Jady Hill. I would have had fewer children.
I won first prize in knitting at the State Fair, and I played bridge
every Tuesday. Before I was born, my grandfather had a nanny
named Eulalia. She raised him. He called her Laly. Bottom line, my friend,
I have earned this plot which you follow.

Leap
Cathy Wittmeyer

Shield your eyes to hang on the last rusty rung of this broken
-open silo. Lake Erie's steel waves ebb to Canada's windmills.

You shouldn't be here.

Balance along the branch to the hay mow hatch. Don't look down.
Pry hinges open. Swing your soft body thru to loose, dusty straw.

You shouldn't be here.

Listen to aging barn beams creaking. Its shoulders shrug under, its
sciatic leans into the blight-spared chestnut. Neither barn nor tree

should be here.

Shards of windows dressed in drapes of cobweb, laced in grain dust,
let light in. A knotted string of baling twine hangs in a loop, and

you shouldn't be here

but you swing thru the chute for the thrill of it, and it isn't the dry
-rotted rope that gives, but the old nail succumbs as you leap free

of all tethers. It seems to last forever. You hear the barn swallow
and that throbbing pulse in your skull on concrete that hums:

you belong right here.

The Stretch Of The Call
Bridget Hayes

Assalatu Khairum-minan-naum. I looked up expecting to see modern speakers on the minaret vibrate with a fuzzy crackle. Instead, I saw the profile of a man on a balcony—a muezzin—reciting the call to prayer against the pinks and blues of a sound-soaked Tunisian desert sky promising the break of day.

From this opening, the muezzin's voice of the old way broke free. Rhythmic in its incantation of animated language, the life behind the words transformed the instant into a rite of being human.

In the developing dawn, there was passion in his song as he lifted the words from his lower abdomen, spiraled them around his torso, wove them through his lungs, rocketed them up his throat, and set their vibrations free into the crisp, clear air. With no hint that he repeated this ritual every day, five times a day, as weeks, months, and years passed by, the melody from this human was fresh and full of life. His call was his prayer as he woke the village, reminding them that prayer was better than sleep. Five bells of mindfulness for the Buddhists, five rings of the clock tower for the secular, and even the alarm of a clock for the atheists, not on the hour, not keeping time, but calibrated with the changing light.

The first time I heard it, I was startled by the sounds mingling with my dreams, echoing, swaying, bouncing from one tower to the next, across the dim lit valleys of the sleepy little town I was in. I awoke just in time to see the sky vibrate the sun into existence. A silver metallic flash in the sky, moving like a minute hand, its particles changed from indigo to plum purple, exploding into splotches and streams of vibrant fiery threads. Red sky in the morning, it was a warning to awaken or miss the restoration to life.

On the edge of the Sahara Desert, in the ancient village of Matmata, I watched as people scrambled from their quiet places to the orange earth street, to the mosque, to somewhere in between. Under the expansive dome of cloudless azure skies, I observed their dedication to the practice of presence. Without trying to understand the stopping of time, the marking of the now, the awakening into all that there is and ever was, the call seeped deeply into my ears.

Over time, I learned to let the words rush through me from head to toe. I learned to slow my footsteps to a standstill. I learned to lift my head to the skies and simply stop. Just for a minute, I would listen, look, and breathe. I learned that the moment, the words, didn't make me think, didn't need me to think, but slowed me, soothed me. Five times a day, the rhythm of the prayer made me be present. The careful drum of Arabic syllables of which I only knew a few words. The voice of a human slinging song with guttural utterances. The stretch of the call across all spaces that humans touched—not forgetting a corner, crack, or closet. This beautiful chant in alignment with the ever-changing cycles of the moon filled up the sky and lit up my eyes.

On the Cover: As I Am
Lizzie Brown

acrylic on canvas, embellished with gold leaf, 24" x 36"

Finding inspiration in kintsugi, the Japanese art of fixing broken ceramics with gold, this painting depicts a woman embracing her flaws and scars, represented by the gold-filled crack down her back. Head lifted and eyes closed, an array of colors ascends from behind her. Her vibrant presence is captivating. Her expression—one of self-acceptance. This painting is a reminder that our imperfections make us beautiful, and our scars tell a story of what we've overcome.

Reflections and ponderings

Contributors were asked how their included creative
nonfiction, poetry, or artwork elevates them and/or their
artistry. Here are their incredible responses.

****

brooklyn baggett, "NAIF CAFE," poetry
"NAIF CAFE," was my first of many poems about Athens, my first
time and first day sitting at a cafe near my hotel. The wildfires of
Evia had just started two days before. I was immediately struck by
the community and conversation of the Athenians around me. The
patrons were discussing the devastation and what they could do
themselves, since the government response was minimal and slow.
As fate would have it, the juxtaposition of the Southern women
behind me, their surface level conversations, embarrassed me as an
American. The rest of my trip continued along the same trajectory,
except it was my own inadequacies that I couldn't help but see. I've
returned to Athens many times, hungry for that community and
authenticity, searching for the heartbeat of the people who are always
pushing me to be a better human.

Ellen Blum Barish, "Reunion," creative nonfiction
When I rediscovered the clay figurine that I made in a high school
art class on a bookshelf at my father's house, it set me on a
journey to break a long-held silence after a terrible car accident.
That journey is detailed in my memoir *Seven Springs*, which was the
most difficult writing project I have ever completed but enabled me
to heal. In "Reunion," I wanted to write about that moment from
the perspective of the figurine. Writing it from a different angle
elevated—and expanded—my sense of the experience and allowed
me to experiment in a new artistic form.

Daisy Bassen, "Thank you to the woman leaning out her window and drumming as we marched for Roe in 2022," poetry
My poem is written to draw strength from the found community beyond those people I know personally. It celebrates a moment of voices raised in an impromptu chorus, lifting up the characters in the poem, the speaker, the author and, I very much hope, the poem's readers. It also literally references "looking up" as well as referencing a Baroque masterpiece.

Elliott batTzedek, "Cicada," poetry
Sometimes, the lives we have built around ourselves are so hardened that they seem unchangeable. Watching cicadas split their skins and appear as completely new creatures with glimmering wings helped me understand that breaking apart is a necessary prequel to radical growth.

Rachel R. Baum, "Over the Rainbow," poetry
This piece elevates my writing by incorporating music into the poem. So much of life is accompanied by music. By using song titles and musical themes, there is an extra element of connection between the writer and the reader. We associate certain songs with people and with our place in time. Music helps to establish a period in history. It can also take the reader into a different dimension, where the words themselves have music. I know that when I wrote "Over the Rainbow," I heard the song in my head as the poetry appeared on the page, and this experience was truly an elevation.

Lizzie Brown, "As I Am," artwork
"As I Am" speaks to my personal journey of rediscovering who I am as a woman. Embracing my shortcomings and flaws, unlearning old habits and beliefs, and becoming more in tune with my purpose and identity has allowed me to understand that I am enough as I am. This awareness, self-discovery, and self-acceptance empowers me to elevate.

Robin Dellabough, "Tap Dancing in Stop & Shop," poetry
Seeing my granddaughter in a joyous moment, despite her family's
struggles, lifted my spirits enormously and inspired this poem.
Taking the risk for the first time to remove all the punctuation raised
my writing practice to a new level. I now feel good and truly elevated!

Michele Evans, "malea," poetry
Simply put, "malea" is a poem about resilience. When I was little,
my mom encouraged my brother and me to write whenever we were
upset about anything. At the time, I was too young to understand
how writing could be therapeutic, but now as an adult, I reach for
a pen, my phone, or my laptop whenever life tries to give me more
than I can handle. While the world today is much different than the
one of my childhood (and yet, in many ways, it is scarily the same),
the one thing that has remained constant for me is using the power
of the written word to deal with life's challenges and circumstances.
The message of "malea" to anyone who is battling insurmountable
obstacles: find your inner strength and never give up.

Jennifer Martinelli Eyre, "If Barbie Were My Daughter," poetry
Writing unveils some of my deepest vulnerabilities, whether I intend
for it to or not. Once I had the first draft of my poem on paper, I
took a step back and reevaluated the message I was trying to convey.
My initial approach to this piece was to call out the unrealistic
beauty standards forced upon women, but what I ended up with
was a quieter promise to a daughter from her mother—a promise
to emulate beauty through love, experiences, and guidance. As I
revised, I realized I had subconsciously embedded fragments of my
experiences and longings into the poem. In weaving pieces of myself
into the words on the page, I risked exposing vulnerabilities, which
was terrifying. But at the same time, freeing. Lifting. Empowering. In
its final version, "If Barbie Were My Daughter" elevated my artistry
into a space where I can share and discover while leaving room for
the reader to do the same. To reach such a space alone is gratifying
but to bring others along with you is pure beauty.

Bridget Hayes, "The Stretch Of The Call," creative nonfiction
"The Stretch Of The Call" is a travel piece—traveling and processing
it through writing elevates my perception. Learning how other
people live in the world opens my mind to how humans are similar
and connected no matter where we are on the planet. I am lifted and
energized by those that I encounter on the road. Traveling offers
my mind endless stimulation and makes me a more flexible and
empathetic person.

Jean Janicke, "Curious Customs of the Dancers of D.C.," poetry
My poem elevates me by capturing how dance lifts my spirits. I
enjoy the music, the movement, and the sisterhood on and off the
stage. I collected snippets for this poem at a dance performance
this summer, and it was so interesting to hear how everyone from
dancers to drummers to professional dancers from Egypt prepared to
go on stage.

Carter Lappin, "pilot," poetry
I believe that this piece elevates my artistry by allowing me to see the
value in abandoning traditional structure and form to best convey a
feeling. Hopefully, this examination of style will carry over into future
writings, causing me to look at the story I want to tell from all angles
instead of sticking to initial instinct.

Rebecca D. Martin, "Girl on the Edge," creative nonfiction
For me, it's all about the songs. I still listen to the Indigo Girls for
that sense of release, and they've added many more albums to their
oeuvre since that "Rites of Passage" concert I attended. But in a sense,
it's about song altogether: as I learn more about my uniquely autistic
self, I see that singing is a stim for me, which means when I sing,
leaning into those harmonies, leaning into the meanings of words
that tell me there are many ways to walk through this world, I release
pent-up energy, I feel lighter, I am elevated. On another level, sharing
this piece is an elevating moment for me. I have felt shame over that
skittle-spinning episode for three decades. Looking at that event

square-on and then sharing it with others gives me power over the shame. It frees me. I hope it might lift others in a similar way.

Glenis Moore, "Escapee," poetry
"Escapee" elevates me and my artistry by showing how common everyday things like a squash plant can surpass all expectations and cheer up an unused part of a garden.

Mary Moreno, "Webb Surfing," poetry
I am basically an upbeat, positive person. But from time to time, I get lost in the news cycle and challenged by anxiety. When I saw the first deep space photo taken by the James Webb space camera, it reinforced the magnificence, the mystery, the beauty of life for me. This poem pretty much wrote itself, my affirmation that there is so much more to life than just the goings-on here on this planet.

Jordan Eve Morral, "Migraine," creative nonfiction
My piece elevates me and, by extension, my artistry by bringing attention to an often-overlooked struggle that I go through. Unless you share in my experience, it is hard to fathom how debilitating a migraine, or any health condition, can be. I could choose to use migraines as an excuse to laze around in bed and accomplish nothing, or I could use my experience to rise above the pain and use it as inspiration and a practice in creativity. My piece is proof of the latter.

Sara Palmer, "Rising to the Occasion," creative nonfiction
I have written creative nonfiction pieces for several blogs, but "Rising to the Occasion" is my first piece in this genre to be published in a literary journal—an artistic elevation resulting in elation! As an older woman who is still "emerging" as a poet and creative writer (after much professional nonfiction writing in the past), it's rewarding to know that my personal experiences are "relatable"—and this encourages me to write more about them. "Rising to the Occasion" is about regaining confidence in my physical abilities after illness, learning to embrace life's pleasures along with its inevitable risks,

and deepening relationships with my adult sons. Reflecting on these experiences in writing was cathartic and emotionally uplifting for me.

Sarah Piper, "Small," poetry
This poem speaks to the unexpected elevation that comes from settling deeply into our lives, even into the challenges and pain points, into the confusion and lostness. In a long and panicked moment of not knowing what to do, I found a fertile unknowing that set me on a different kind of exploration of life—one that doesn't need so many answers, but feels generally open to being surprised by a day. It's not always as easy as that, of course, but this poem reflects how the spirit of us rises when we let ourselves more fully inhabit life's smallest days.

Shieva Salehnia, "Baptism," poetry
My piece elevates me because it serves as a reminder that I belong in the world, that I am part of nature, and that nature is all around us, even in the middle of a metropolis.

Susan Shea, "Repast," poetry
"Repast" elevated me by making me embrace aging with joy and fellowship.

Morgan Sheehan, "On the mats," creative nonfiction
For me, writing and jiu-jitsu operate in a similar way. Both are about joy. Both share pieces of myself that are not always open to the light. And, ideally, through both we form community.

Tramaine Suubi, "begin again," poetry
My piece elevated me by lifting me out of a deeply unhealthy mental space during my undergraduate studies. This poem was a way of affirming myself the way I wanted to be affirmed. I am indebted to this piece and poetry as a whole.

Annabelle Taghinia, "To Forgive You," poetry
This piece is an example of how writing has helped me reflect on my own emotions and detangle them. The poem deals with forgiveness and letting go, two processes that writing taught me how to do.

Bethany Tap, "This is a poem about birth trauma," poetry
This poem is very meta. It's a poem about processing trauma written as a way to process trauma. It plays with the idea of hiding trauma behind the pretense of art, even as the art itself provides a means to lift up the trauma and acknowledge it for what it is. Writing it was an act of elevating my own experience and giving it validity.

Angelica Terso, "Anatomy of a Lumpia Girl," creative nonfiction
When I look up the definition of the word elevate, it's described as "to move or raise to a higher place or position"; "lift up"; and "to raise to a higher state." A couple of months ago, I was talking to a friend and I casually mentioned how I could never write creative nonfiction pieces, and how it's brave for other writers to do so, being that whatever their subject or inspiration is, would surely be close to them. What a vulnerable thing to share any type of writing, let alone something so real. It wasn't until I attended a workshop that I ever considered it, and when I saw Yellow Arrow Publishing's post on social media about this issue, I knew it was meant for me to finally share this story. I wrote "Anatomy of a Lumpia Girl" in hopes to put into words what I was never able to during those trying years. Doing so allowed me to be "raised to a higher state," emotionally, spiritually, and artistically. And I thank Yellow Arrow for that.

Ann Weil, "Your Daddy Comes Back as a Monarch," poetry
In this poem, I wanted to honor my deceased ex-husband. We had a great love for a very long time, and he is the father of my children. He was greatly concerned about the declining monarch butterfly population and had planted milkweed and other plants attractive to this species to try and help. After he died, the kids and I decided that anytime we saw a monarch, we'd know it was the embodiment of his

spirit. When grieving a loss, I find solace in working on my hands and knees in my garden. This is a poem of homage to a healing pastime and a good man. Gratitude for both elevates me.

Melanie Weldon-Soiset, "Lullaby as Lament," poetry
"Lullaby as Lament" elevates common losses, including even the loss of language. As a self-erasure, "Lullaby as Lament" throws the first cry of a lament into the air; some of the words then float away. The portion that responds to the tug of gravity, now reduced, nonetheless reveals new possibilities, new links. "Lullaby as Lament" explores the risk and potential of vertical connection, even as it seeks to lace horizontally with other singers.

Samantha Liana Williams, "An Extenuation of Thanks," poetry
I keep going back to this, but every artist, every person has a well of experiences, feelings, memories, etc. And for a writer, this never ending well or archive allows us to pull out different experiences and meld them together with what we might be currently feeling or take more than one experience and meld it with another. This poem is one of those poems melded together from different memories and feelings and pieced back together. So for me this poem feels very in tune with my artistry because it is a piece that's been carefully reflected on with stillness and intentionality.

Cathy Wittmeyer, "Leap," poetry
The origins of this poem "Leap" began with the thought, *what does "on top of the world" feel like*? I live in the Alps so the thought comes to me often at high elevations, and I wondered when I would have had a similar feeling before I moved here. As I wrote, another question arose, and my level of consciousness about places was elevated.

Contributors

brooklyn baggett is a trans poet and artist living in New York. she holds an MFA from Goddard College and teaches workshops on tactile poetry. her work has appeared in *samfiftyfour*, *Yellow Arrow Journal*, *the engine(idling*, *Impossible Archetype*, *Big Muddy*, and *River Styx*. brooklyn's chapbook *we cast shadows & other true stories* (2023) is available from Bottlecap Press. she is also the founder and managing editor of new words {press} - a trans and gender-expansive poetry and hybrid poetry journal.

Ellen Blum Barish is author of the memoir *Seven Springs* (Shanti Arts, 2021) and *Views from the Home Office Window: On Motherhood, Family and Life* (Adams Street Publishing, 2007) and a contributor to two anthologies published by Chicago Story Press. Her essays can be found in *Brevity*, *Lilith*, *Literary Mama*, *Full Grown People*, *Five Minutes*, *Tablet*, and *The New Times Tiny Love Stories* and heard on Chicago Public Radio.

Daisy Bassen is a poet and community child psychiatrist who graduated from Princeton University's Creative Writing Program and completed her medical training at the University of Rochester and Brown University. Her work has been published in *Salamander*, *McSweeney's*, *Smartish Pace*, *Plume*, and *[PANK]*, among other journals. She was the winner of the So to Speak 2019 Poetry Contest, the 2019 ILDS White Mice Contest, the 2020 Beullah Rose Poetry Prize, and the 2022 Erskine J. Poetry Prize. She lives in Rhode Island with her family. Her fiction is represented by Jennifer Lyons of Jennifer Lyons Agency.

Elliott batTzedek is a Pushcart Prize nominated poet and liturgist. She is the recipient of the Robert Bly translation prize, judged by Martha Collins, and a Leeway Foundation Art and Change Award. She works in four slightly different parts of the bookselling industry and also as a liturgist for Jewish communities across the U.S. Her poems and translations have been published in *American Poetry Review, Massachusetts Review, Broadkill Review, Lilith, I-70 Review, Hunger Mountain Review, Sakura Review, Apiary, Cahoodaloodaling, Naugatuck River Review, Poemeleon, Philadelphia Stories*, and a Split This Rock poem of the week. Her chapbook *the enkindled coal of my tongue* (2017) was published by Wicked Banshee Press. A chapbook of translations of *A Necklace of White Pearls* by Shez is forthcoming from Moonstone Press in 2024.

Rachel R. Baum is a Best of the Net nominated poet and the editor of *Funeral and Memorial Service Readings, Poems and Tributes* (McFarland, 1999). She is the founder of Moving Mountains Poets and the Saratoga Peace Pod, crafters who create warm items for families in crisis. Her poems have been published in *OneArt, Jewish Literary Journal, The Phare, Raven's Perch, New Verse News*, and others. She has two poetry chapbooks: *Richard Brautigan's Concussion* (Bottlecap Press, 2023) and *How to Rob a Convenience Store* (Cowboy Jamboree Press, 2024). Rachel lives in Saratoga Springs, New York, with her dog, Tennyson.

Lizzie Brown is a Richmond-based artist and owner of From The Core Art Studio. She is a Virginia Commonwealth University alumna with a dual degree in painting and art education, and a minor in art history. Lizzie has been displaying her work in galleries and spaces throughout the southeastern states, Washington, D.C., and Maryland, vending at pop-up markets in surrounding areas and leading art experiences and camps for youth. Lizzie's connection to creating and teaching are a form of ministry. She creates colorful portraits depicting the beauty, resilience, and vibrancy of African American men, women, and children.

Robin Dellabough is a poet and writer with a master's from the University of California, Berkeley, Journalism School. *Double Helix* (2022) is her debut collection and includes a Pushcart Prize nominated poem. Recent poems have appeared or are forthcoming in *Rattle, Gyroscope, Yellow Arrow Journal, Stoneboat, Halfway Down the Stairs, Mom Egg Review, Blue Unicorn, Negative Capability*, and other publications and anthologies.

Michele Evans, a fifth-generation Washingtonian (D.C.), is a writer, high school English teacher, and adviser for her school's literary magazine, *Unbound*. Despite always wearing the color black, she exhibits a certain fondness for blueberries, blue hydrangeas, blues musicians, and Blue Mountain coffee. This 2023 Pushcart Prize nominee and winner of the ASP Bulletin poetry contest has been published in *Artemis, Maryland Literary Review, Sky Island Journal, The Write Launch*, and elsewhere. *purl*, her debut collection of poetry, is forthcoming from Finishing Line Press in 2025. You can find her at awordsmithie.com or on Instagram @awordsmithie.

Jennifer Martinelli Eyre graduated with her MFA in writing from the Vermont College of Fine Arts (VCFA) in January 2023. She spent her time at VCFA studying writing for children and young adults but remains drawn to various genres, particularly free verse poetry. When Jennifer is not writing, you can usually find her behind a desk at her full-time job or reading one of the many books piled on her nightstand. Jennifer has resided in Maryland her entire life; she currently lives in Forest Hill with her husband, daughter, and ornery cat who enjoys walking across keyboards.

Bridget Hayes lives in Sonoma County, California, with her wife and two orange cats. Her work is forthcoming in *Ginosko Literary Journal, Wild Roof Journal*, and *The Letters Home Collection*. She has won first place, second place, and fourth place ribbons for her poetry at the Sonoma County Fair. She is a member of the International Women's Writing Guild and the Redwood Writers Club.

Elizabeth Hill was a finalist in the 2022 Rattle Poetry Contest, with her poem also appearing as Poem of the Day on February 20, 2023. She was also nominated for the 2023 Pushcart Prize by the *Last Stanza Poetry Journal*. Her poetry has been published in *34th Parallel Magazine, SAND, Boomerlit,* and *Catamaran,* among other journals. Elizabeth is a retired Administrative Law judge who was responsible for suits concerning learning disabled children. She lives in Harlem, New York, with her husband and two irascible cats.

Jean Janicke is a blind economist, coach, dancer, and writer. She lives in Washington, D.C., and enjoys getting out of the city to the mountains of central Virginia. Her work has appeared in *Mocking Heart Review, Rabbit,* and *Creation.*

Carter Lappin is a Californian author who usually writes fiction. Her works have appeared in publications such as *Sunlight Press, Apparition Lit, Manawaker Studio,* and *Word Balloon Books.* You can find her on Twitter @CarterLappin.

Rebecca D. Martin lives in central Virginia with her husband and daughters. Her essays and poems have been published in the *Curator,* the Brevity blog, *Isele,* and *Taproot,* among others. She is currently at work on an autism memoir filled with houses and books and can be found at rebeccadmartin.substack.com, where she talks about some of her favorite things, including books, poetry, and neurodiversity.

Glenis Moore is a relatively new poet working in the flat lands of the Fens near Cambridge, United Kingdom. When she is not writing she makes beaded jewelery, knits, reads, and runs 10K races slowly. She has been previously published in *Sequoia Speaks, Cosmic Daffodil Journal, Constellations,* and *Impspired.*

Mary Moreno is both a musician and a writer. Her career bridges both worlds—each inspiring the other—and her work includes fiction, nonfiction, poetry, songs, and contemporary chamber music ensembles, as well as electronic music. She has been recognized by the New York Foundation for the Arts, National League of American Pen Women, and the Elaine Kaufman Table 4 Foundation, and her work has been published by *Skyhorse*, *Level Best Books*, and *Oberon Poetry Journal*.

Jordan Eve Morral is a simple girl who spends her time reading, writing, and drinking peppermint tea. She is a graduate of Pennsylvania State University where she received a bachelor's degree in English with a minor in writing and digital media. Most of her writings focus on the beauty of the mundane and the meaning created through impermanence. She is an emerging voice who plans to put more of herself out into the world.

Sara Palmer is a retired psychologist and the author of four nonfiction books published in the Johns Hopkins Press Health Books series. Since retirement, she has written poetry and short prose pieces. Her work has appeared in *Yellow Arrow Journal*, *Pen in Hand*, *The Ekphrastic Review*, and *Persimmon Tree*, and in two multi-author collections, *Fractured Hearts: Multi-faith Words of Hope and Healing* and *Poetry is Life: Writing with Yellow Arrow*. She lives in Baltimore, Maryland.

Sarah Piper is a writer and physician living in the San Francisco Bay area. Words are a favorite medicine, and she writes to map the contours of health and illness, to nourish small delights, to push out on tight walls, and to log life lessons from insects in the garden. Her previous work can be read in the **KINDLING** issue of *Yellow Arrow Journal* and on her website for invisible illness advocacy at hopetripping.com.

Shieva Salehnia, raised in South Dakota by Iranian-immigrant parents, is a writer and attorney. She pulls much inspiration from the lyrical traditions of the SWANA region and contemporary American poetry and prose. Shieva uses poetry to define and redefine the self, as a means of liberation, and to allow others to feel less alone in their own uncommon and mundane experiences. She currently lives in Los Angeles, California, where she coedits the literary zine *Embryo Concepts* and is working on a comic series called *Girl Crazy* about the adventures of two queer women living in New York City.

Jennifer N. Shannon has published three books: *Silent Teardrops*; *for the LOVE, short stories and poems, vol. 1*; and *for the LOVE, short stories and poems, vol. 2.* Her poetry, short stories, photographs, and essays have been in an anthology and literary magazines, including *North Dakota Quarterly, Yellow Arrow Journal, Deep South Magazine, Auburn Avenue*, and others. Jennifer was a 2022 Baker Artist Awards finalist, a poetry fellow at the Watering Hole, and in 2023, she was selected as a Maryland State Arts Council Triennial Artist for Literary Arts. Jennifer is a proud South Carolinian and Gamecock who lives in Maryland with her son and fiancé. Visit jennifernshannon.com or follow her @writerjns on Instagram and Facebook.

Susan Shea is a retired school psychologist who was raised in New York City and now lives in a forest in Pennsylvania. In the past year, since she returned to writing poetry, more than one hundred of her poems have been accepted by a number of publications, including *Across the Margin, Ekstasis, Feminine Collective, The Avalon Literary Review, Persimmon Tree Literary Magazine, Military Experience and the Arts, Triggerfish Critical Review, Amethyst Review, Litbreak Magazine, A Time of Singing, Invisible City,* and others.

Morgan Sheehan is an educator, writer, and Brazilian jiu-jitsu competitor. She lives in western Massachusetts with her fabulous family and small flock of Pekin ducks. She loves words, gardening, and sparring with friends in the gym.

Tramaine Suubi is a multilingual writer from Kampala, Uganda. They earned their BA in philosophy and French. Later on, they earned their MFA from the Iowa Writers' Workshop. Their words live in *Brink*, *Solstice*, and other spaces. Tramaine is the managing editor of Writivism and is officially represented by the Creative Arts Agency. Their first and second books will be published by Amistad, an imprint of HarperCollins. Tramaine is in love with all things water.

Annabelle Taghinia is a writer from New England. She is currently a sophomore in high school and spends her free time working on short fiction pieces and poems, including a collection of stories of Persian women. She enjoys reading poetry collections, realistic fiction, and magical realism. This is her first publication.

Bethany Tap received her MFA in creative writing from the University of North Carolina at Wilmington. Her work has recently been published or is forthcoming in *Flash Fiction Magazine*, *ballast*, *The MacGuffin*, *Emerge Literary Journal*, *Thimble Literary Magazine*, *The Hyacinth Review*, *Flash Frontier*, and *Cosmic Daffodil Journal*, among others. She lives in Grand Rapids, Michigan, with her wife and four kids.

Angelica Terso (she/her) is a Filipino American writer currently residing in Maryland. Her stories feature LGBT, Asian Americans, and other under-represented themes. Previously, her work has appeared in *Atticus Review*, *The Raven Review*, and others. When she's not writing, reading, or daydreaming, she's either hiking or rock climbing. You can find her on Instagram @angelicatersowrites.

Ann Weil is the author of *Lifecycle of a Beautiful Woman* (Yellow Arrow Publishing, 2023) and *Blue Dog Road Trip* (Gnashing Teeth Publishing, 2024). Her poetry has been nominated for the Pushcart Prize and Best of the Net and appears in *Pedestal Magazine, DMQ Review, Maudlin House, 3Elements Review, Okay Donkey, SWWIM Every Day, The Shore*, and elsewhere. She earned her doctorate at the University of Michigan and lives in Ann Arbor, Michigan, and Key West, Florida.

Melanie Weldon-Soiset's poetry lives in *Sunlight Press, Clerestory,* and others. A 2022 Washington Writers' Publishing House contest winner, Melanie is a #ChurchToo survivor, contemplative prayer leader, and poetry editor at *Geez Magazine*. Melanie is also a highly sensitive person (HSP) who struggles with insomnia, yet values insights gained through dreaming. She enjoys the brown thrasher bird song before dawn. Melanie is from Georgia, land of Muscogee and Cherokee, and she currently lives in Washington, D.C., on Nacotchtank territory. Find Melanie in real life biking on local greenways. Find her online (including her poetry and prayer missive) at melanieweldonsoiset.com or on Instagram @MelanieWelSoi.

Samantha Liana Williams is a writer and poet. Her work about two-ness and nostalgic reflections has been seen in *BlackJoy Archive, Obsidian Literature,* and *Soft Quarterly*. She is a poetry reader for *Muzzle Magazine*. She is also a 2023 recipient of the John Lewis Writing Grant for poetry. She lives in Atlanta, Georgia, with her eight-year-old daughter and newborn.

Cathy Wittmeyer, from western New York, hosts the Word to Action retreat in the Alps where poets stitch science onto beautiful words to create optimistic poems for the planet. She loves leading poetry workshops where discovery inspires hope in response to fear. Editor of the anthology *Eden is a Backyard: Climate poems from Word to Action* from Edition Eupolinos, her work has also appeared in *Superpresent*, *Ekphrastic Review*, and *Book of Matches*, among others, and a short poem won an honorable mention in the 1982 Erie County SPCA poster contest.